ART & DESIGN CAREERS

A Career in ILLUSTRATION

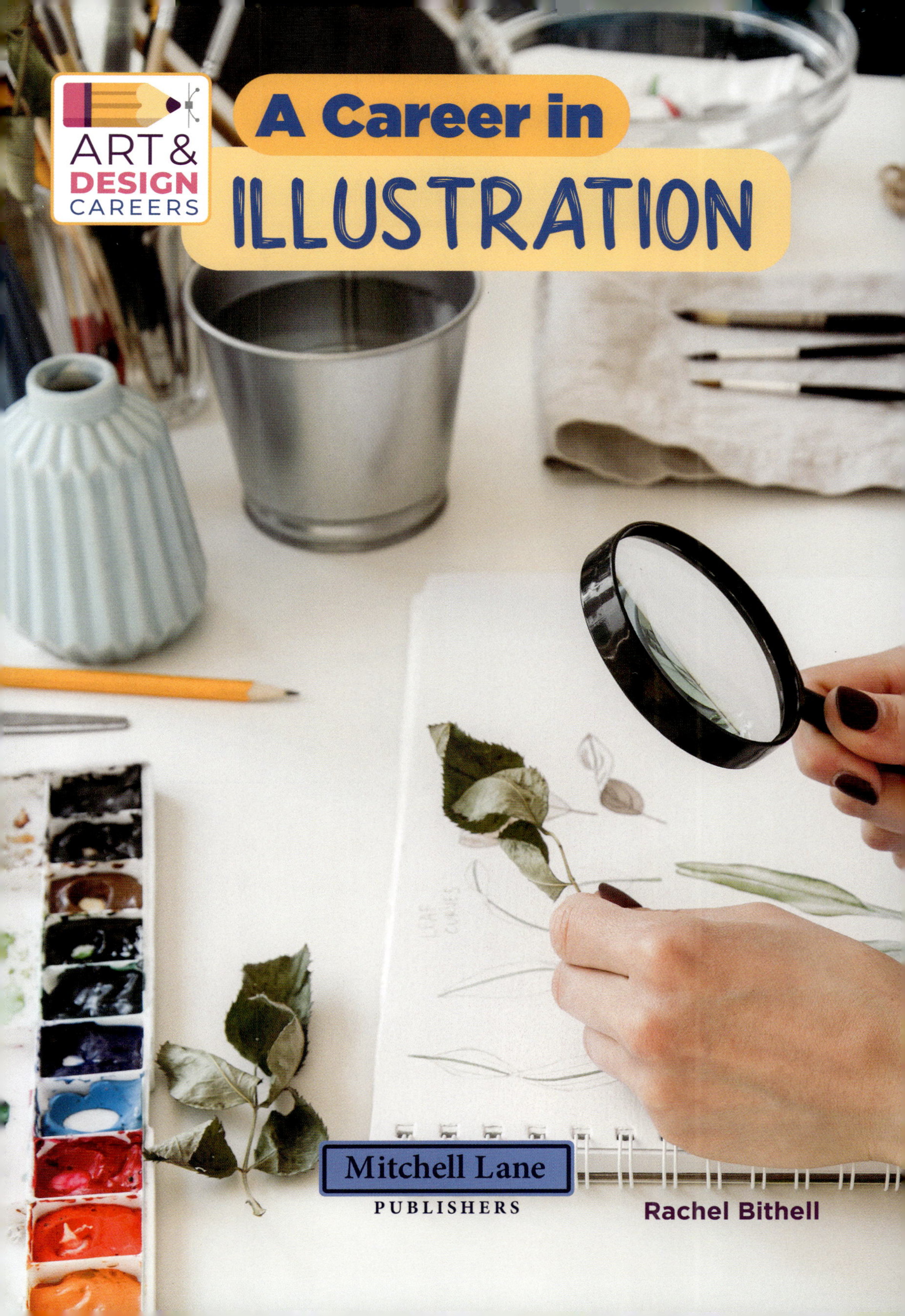

Mitchell Lane
PUBLISHERS

Rachel Bithell

Mitchell Lane
PUBLISHERS

mitchelllanepub.com

2001 SW 31st Avenue
Hallandale, FL 33009

First Edition, 2026.
Author: Rachel Bithell
Designer: Ed Morgan
Editor: Tammy Gagne

Series: Art and Design Careers
Title: A Career in Illustration

Library bound ISBN: 979-8-89260-504-5
eBook ISBN: 979-8-89260-507-6

Photo credits: cover, contents, p. 5, 7, 11, 13, 21, 23, 29, 31, 35, 37, 39, 41, 43 freepik.com; p. 9, 15, 17, 19, 25, 27, 33 Shutterstock

Contents

Chapter One

Thinking in Pictures

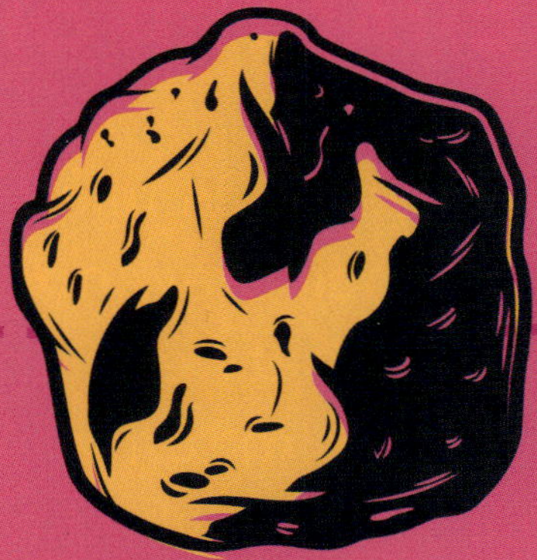

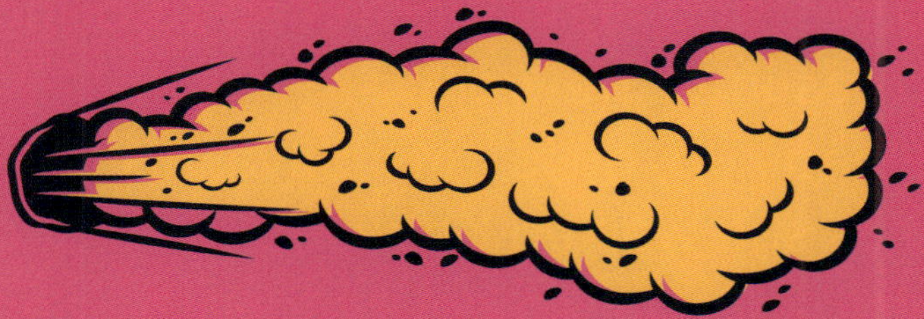

Alex flipped through his science notebook. He knew he had written down the differences between asteroids and comets. He needed those notes for the worksheet he was trying to finish before the bell rang.

"There," Alex whispered as he spotted his drawings. An icy comet, its tail streaming behind, hurtled through space next to a rocky asteroid in a tidy orbit around the sun.

CHAPTER ONE

Alex's notebook was filled with his doodles and pencil drawings. Squeezed into margins and between lines, the drawings helped him remember information. His brain liked to think in pictures, and his fingers liked to bring those pictures into the world.

"Heads up, guys," Ms. Silva, his teacher, said as she walked between rows of desks. "Quick announcement before the period ends. The community center is having a book drive. They want children's books to use in their after-school program. If anyone has some gently used ones at home, maybe something you've outgrown, you can donate them to a . . ."

The bell interrupted her just as she came to Alex's desk.

"Good cause," she resumed. "I'll have a donation box outside the classroom door starting tomorrow!" she called over the buzz of kids talking as they stashed their stuff in backpacks. She spotted Alex's notes before he could close his book.

Thinking in Pictures

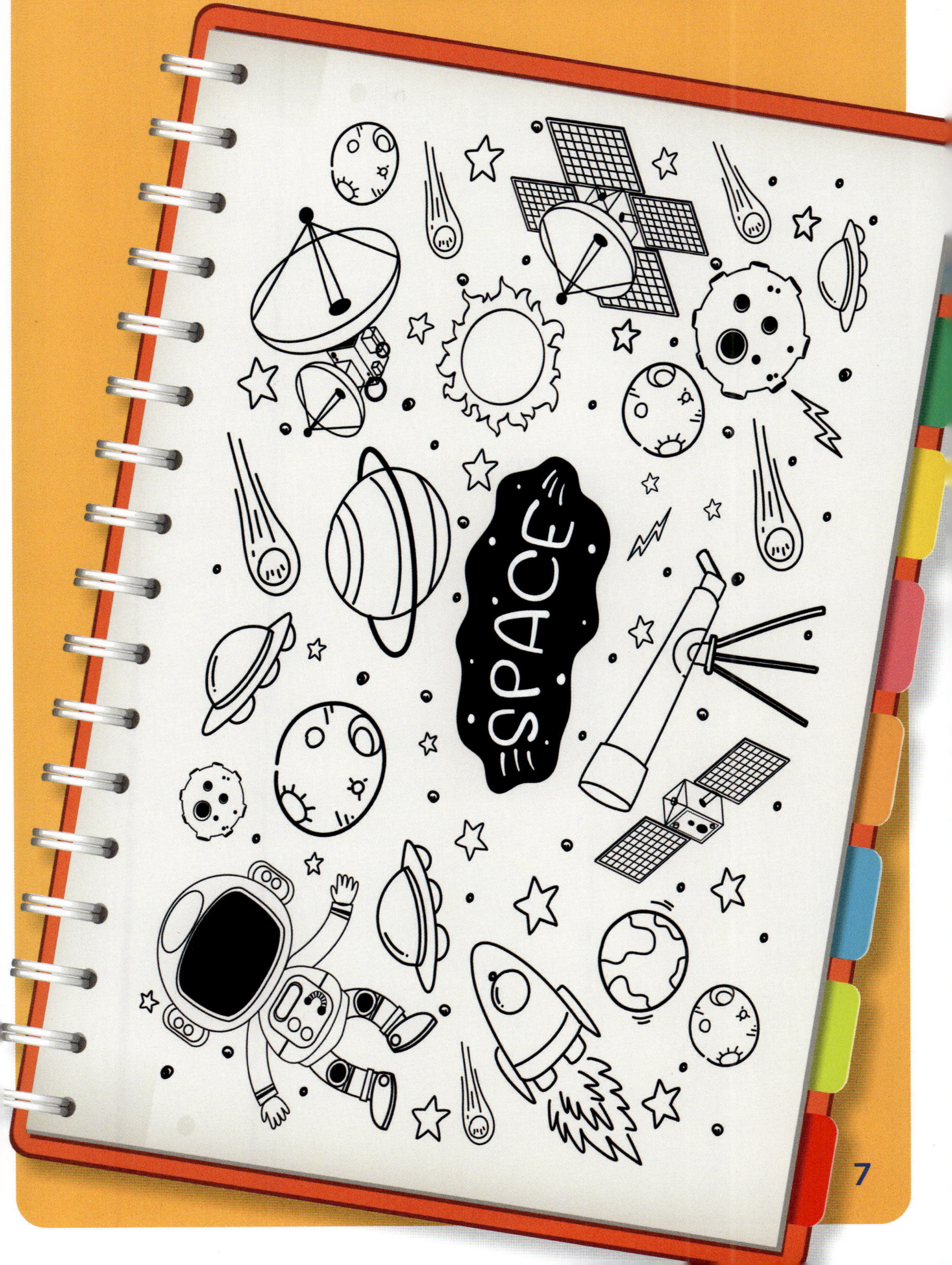

"Did you draw all of those?" she asked him.

Alex nodded, a little worried. He didn't want her to think he was drawing instead of paying attention in class. But she smiled.

"I'm impressed," she said. "You're very talented."

In his bedroom that night, Alex flipped through the books on his shelf, remembering Ms. Silva's words about the book drive, as well as her encouraging words about his drawings. Among his fantasy books and graphic novels, there were many picture books he had loved as a little kid. They were stories he'd read again and again.

He opened his favorite. He still remembered all the words. But it was the pictures that spoke to his heart. When he was a child, they brought him into a world where imagined things became real, and monsters could be his best friends. He was torn between wanting to keep the book and wanting to share it with other kids.

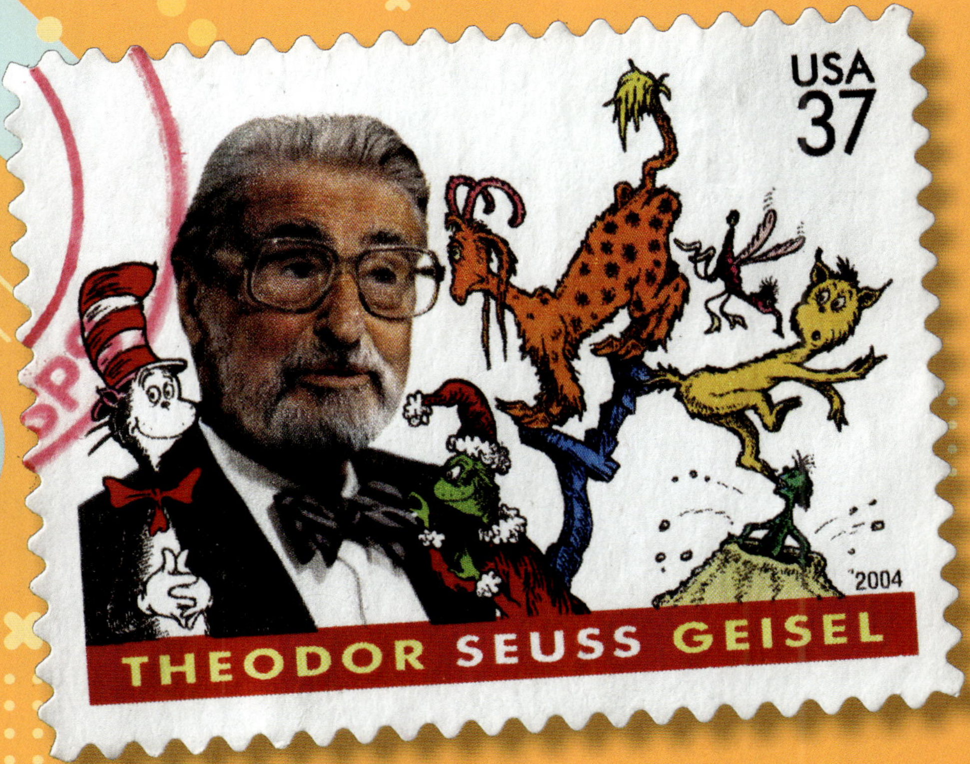

Two Jobs in One

Authors and illustrators often work together on projects such as picture books. Often, a publisher will pair an artist with an author to add graphic images to a story. Sometimes, one person performs both the writing and the drawing. Dr. Seuss, Jan Brett, and Maurice Sendak all wrote and illustrated their own books.

He ran a finger over an **illustration** of the main character.

Could I draw this? he wondered.

He set to work at his desk, where paper and pencils were always handy. Soon his pencil sketch was complete. It begged to be brought to life with color. He considered watercolors before grabbing colored pencils. They would be faster. He examined his finished character.

Not exactly like the picture in the book. But more my style, he thought.

He tried again with the character in a different pose, a new expression on his face. This time he imagined a setting and added a background.

Pretty good! Maybe I could be an illustrator, he pondered.

The next day, Alex deposited a stack of books into Ms. Silva's box. He hoped they would bring smiles to other kids. But his favorite was waiting safely on his shelf at home. If becoming an illustrator was in his future, he would need lots of practice.

Thinking in Pictures

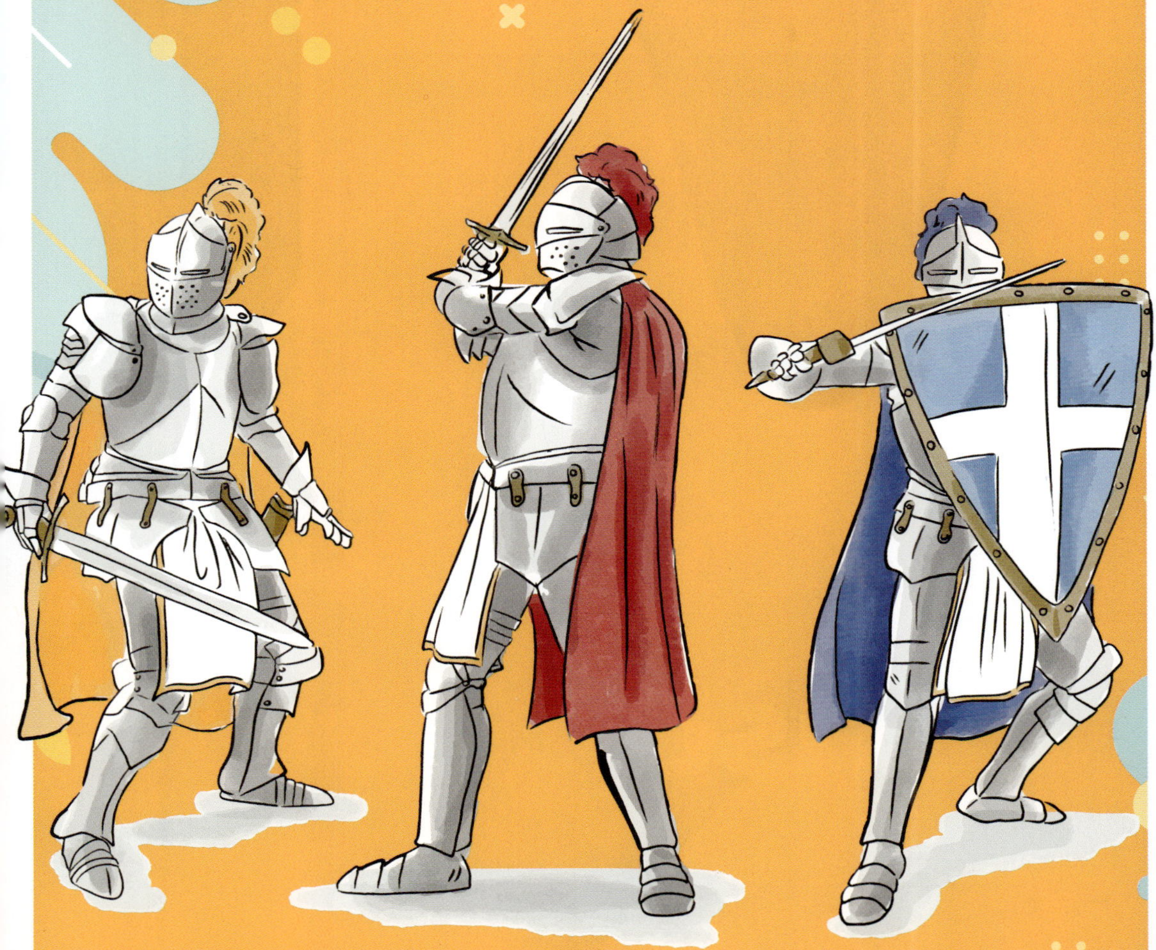

Chapter Two

The History of Illustration

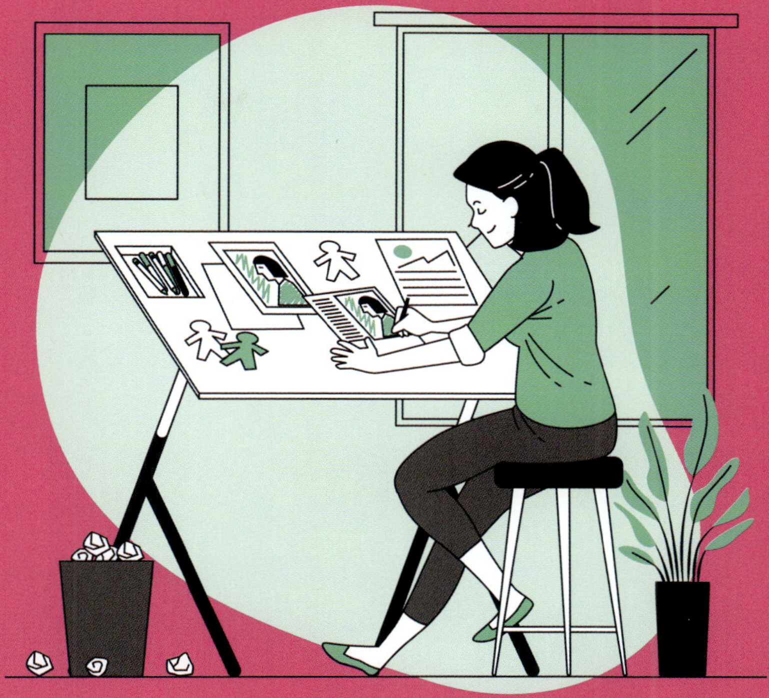

Illustration is art that tells a story. It explains, extends, or decorates text. Most children's books, greeting cards, and instruction manuals feature illustrations. They make the text more interesting or clearer.

The art of illustration is ancient. It is even older than written language. Cave paintings in Lascaux, France, are about nineteen thousand years old. That makes them the oldest known illustrations.

CHAPTER TWO

Artists in ancient Greece and Rome added illustrations to pottery. Often, they **depicted** stories about heroes or gods. Starting around 1100 CE, Chinese painters decorated the covers of books. In the Middle Ages, monks in Europe spent their lives making religious books by hand. The monks similarly decorated these books with illustrations.

Around 1440, Johannes Gutenberg invented a printing press with moveable type. The machine allowed illustrations to be added to a printed page. Artists carved the illustrations into wood or metal plates. The illustrated text could be mass produced.

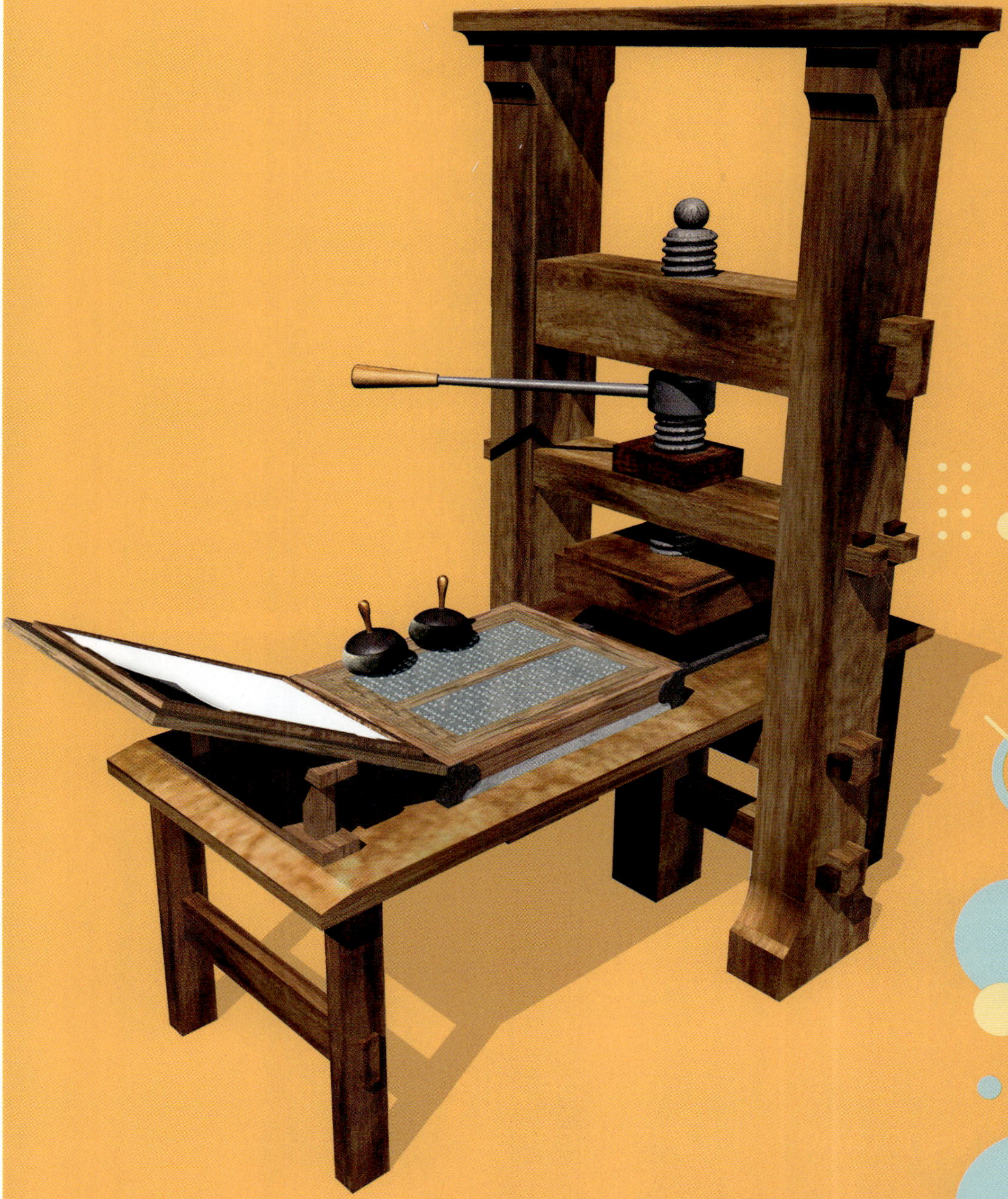

Printing presses, like this early Gutenberg press, helped make illustration a way to earn a living.

CHAPTER TWO

By the 1700s, printers made illustrated newspapers, flyers, and books for both children and adults. For some artists, illustrating became a way to make a living. In the 1800s and 1900s, advances in color printing made illustration even more popular among both artists and shoppers.

In 1901, the United Kingdom's Beatrix Potter published *The Tale of Peter Rabbit*. The book's success was due largely to Potter's charming illustrations. Potter was also an **entrepreneur**. She sold stuffed toys and games based on her books. Peter Rabbit became one of the first illustrated characters made into merchandise.

In the United States, the popularity of illustrations soared from about 1880 to 1940. Artists produced inventive and skilled work. One of the best-known illustrators of this era was Norman Rockwell. His scenes and portraits of ordinary people touched generations of Americans.

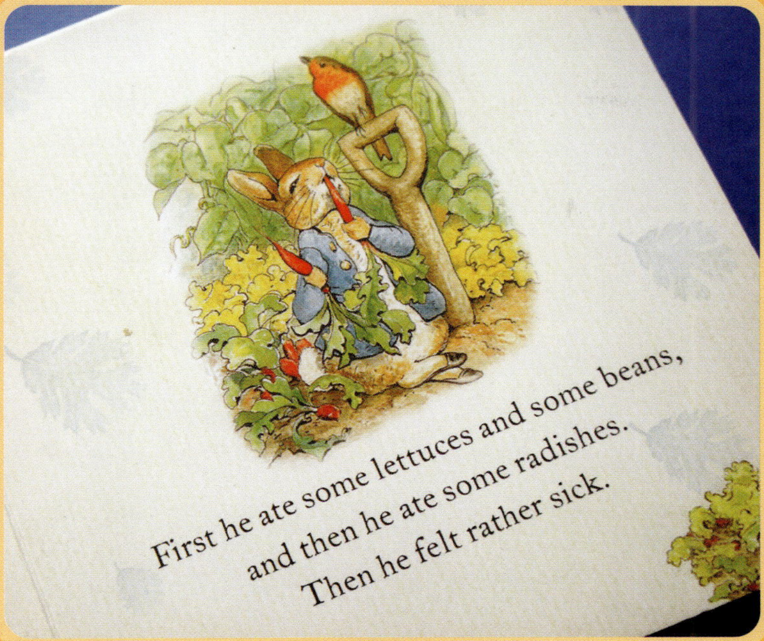

Celebrating Potter

The year 2016 marked the 150th anniversary of Beatrix Potter's birth. The United Kingdom released postage stamps for the event. They featured six of Potter's best-loved characters, such as Peter Rabbit and Benjamin Bunny. The same year, a first edition copy of *The Tale of Peter Rabbit* sold for £43,000. That is equal to about $56,000.

CHAPTER TWO

Some of today's most famous illustrators work in children's publishing. For example, Mo Willems' *Pigeon* series has sold more than six million copies and been published in twenty languages. The Caldecott Medal is awarded yearly for excellence in illustration for children's literature. In 2024, the medal went to Vashti Harrison. She is the first Black woman to win the honor.

Today, illustrators can work in many fields. They make art for stationery, books, magazine features, graphic novels, and comics. Artists also illustrate for the fashion industry and scientific publications. Illustrators capture scenes from inside courtrooms, where cameras are sometimes banned. Many companies hire illustrators to create product packaging, advertising, and instruction manuals.

Illustrator Chris Russell is hopeful about the future of his profession. In a blog for the *Lit Hub* website, he wrote that e-books and digital publishing have "rekindled the **bibliophile**'s interest in the book as a physical object of beauty."

The History of Illustration

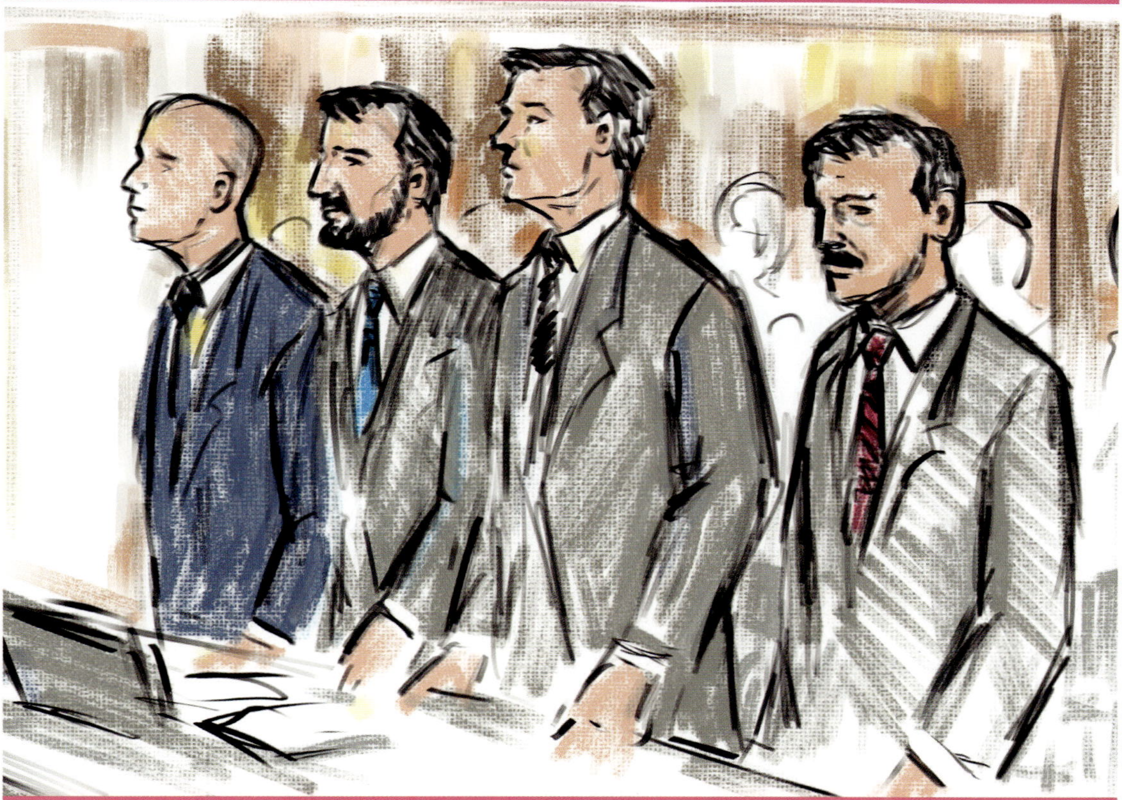

Courtroom illustrations show the public scenes from important trials where cameras are not always allowed.

Chapter Three

An Illustrator's Tool Kit

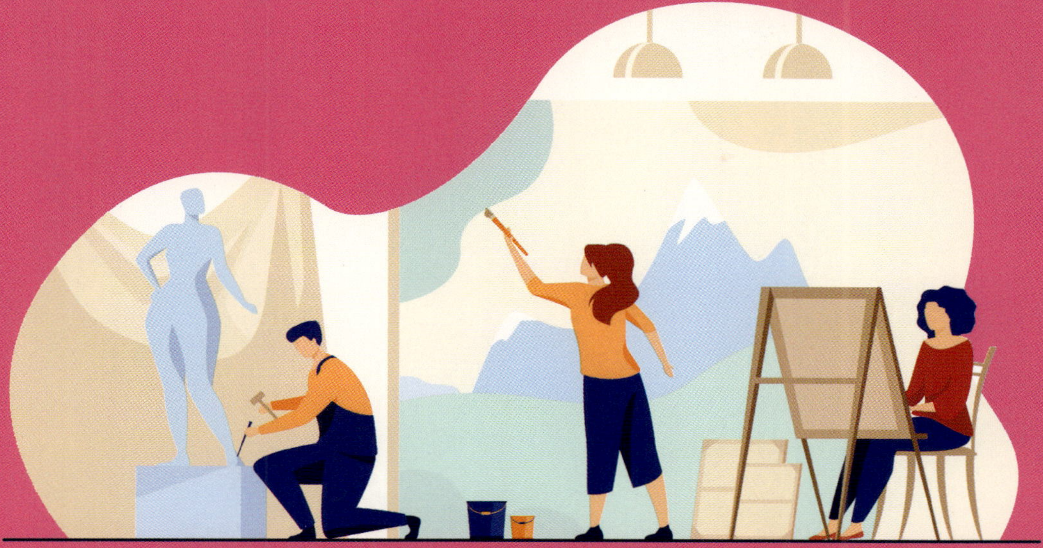

Illustrators are artists. They must be skilled in at least one type of two-dimensional, or flat, art. This could be drawing, painting, printmaking, or collage work. They might use traditional **media**, such as oil paints, pencils, and watercolors. Or they might work entirely on a computer to make digital art. Many illustrators mix more than one medium. No matter how they make their art, successful illustrators always have a distinct style.

CHAPTER THREE

Currently, almost all printing is done with computers. Even art that is created by hand must be scanned or photographed and turned into a computer file. Then editors and designers can more easily make changes and add text.

Illustrators have different opinions about the value of a college degree in art. An art program is a chance to learn new skills and try new methods and styles. Peers and teachers can provide feedback. And students often meet people working in the field. Illustrator Darrell Rees says his college connections launched his career. He writes in his book *How to Be an Illustrator*, "By the time I left college I had already received seven **commissions**, with each one generating more work."

An Illustrator's Tool Kit

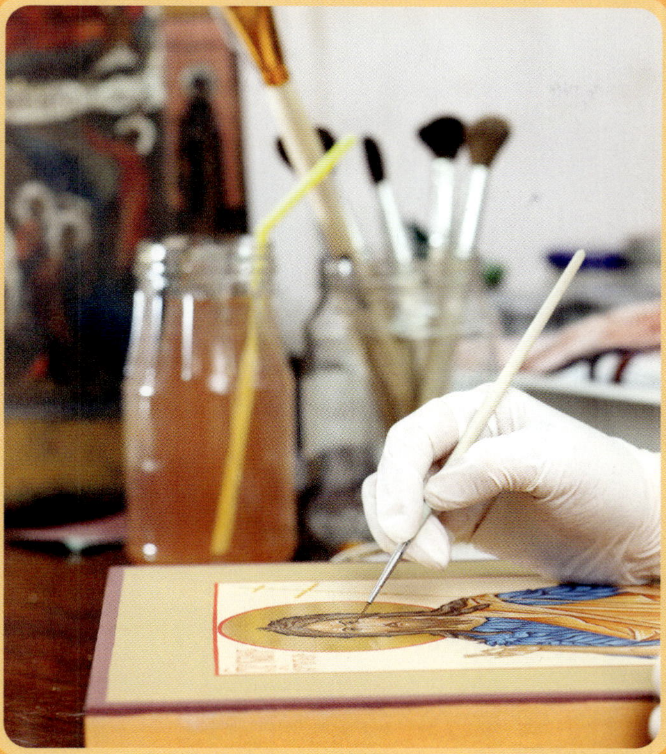

The Cost of Art School

Many public colleges in the United States offer respected degrees in art. Public colleges get some of their funding from the state in which they are located. Residents of that state pay less than other people to attend. For these in-state students, programs can cost a fraction of the price of a private art school.

Degrees, however, are expensive. Students often take on debt to pay for art school. And beginning illustrators usually do not make much money. That can make it hard to pay off loans. Also, a degree is not required to work in the field. Stan Yan has been writing and illustrating for more than a dozen years. In an interview for this book, he said, "Not once has a client, editor, or art director asked to see my diploma, only my **portfolio**."

Beginning illustrators who do not go to college must learn and make connections in other ways. They can find classes and workshops online or in person. Many fields have professional groups. The Society of Children's Book Writers and Illustrators and the Association of Medical Illustrators are examples. These groups offer current information about their field. Often, they hold classes and conferences. They are also a place to meet other illustrators and get feedback.

An Illustrator's Tool Kit

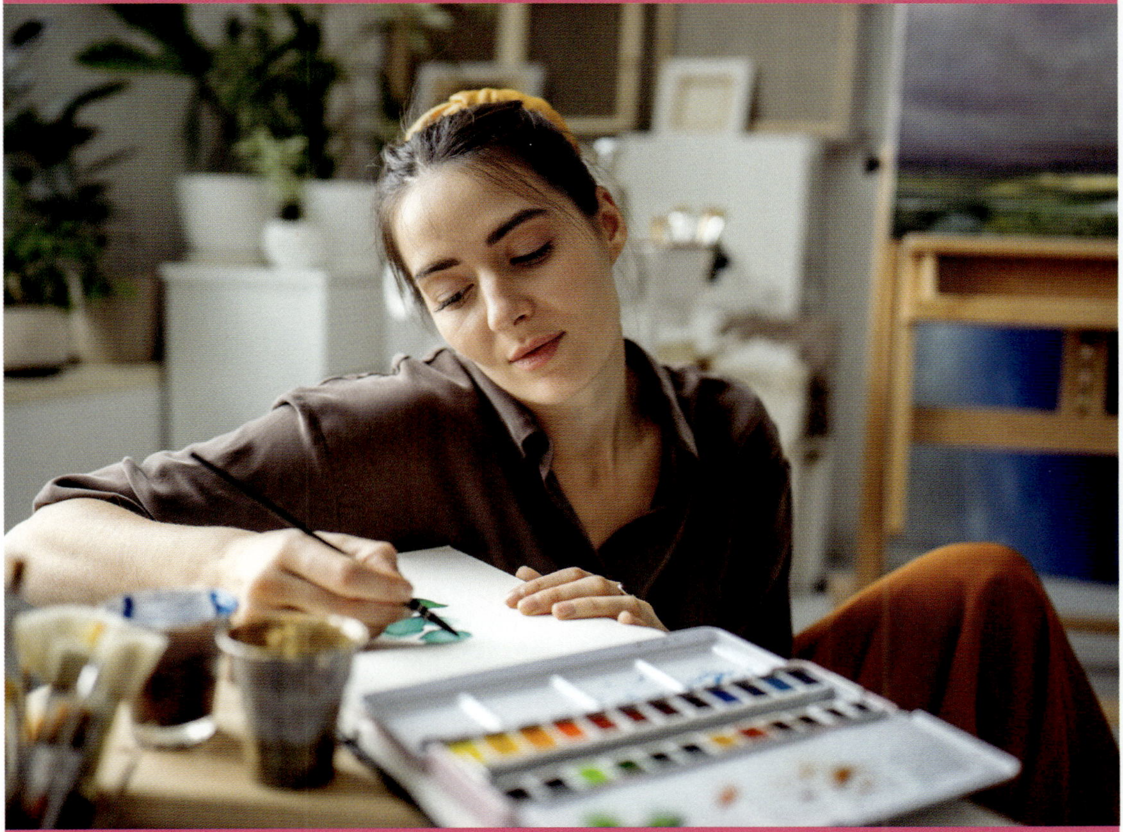

While most artists create their work alone, connections in the field are important for a successful career.

Illustrators in some fields need more specific training. Medical illustrators must have a degree in a science-related field. Court room illustrators need to understand the legal system and legal terms. Fashion illustrators need to know the process for making clothes.

In all fields, it is helpful to know how to use at least one type of art software. Procreate is a popular choice among illustrators. Adobe's group of programs, called Creative Cloud, is also widely used. These programs can be pricey. But sometimes students can get discounts. One free option is Krita. This program can be a good choice for young people who want to try out digital art.

An Illustrator's Tool Kit

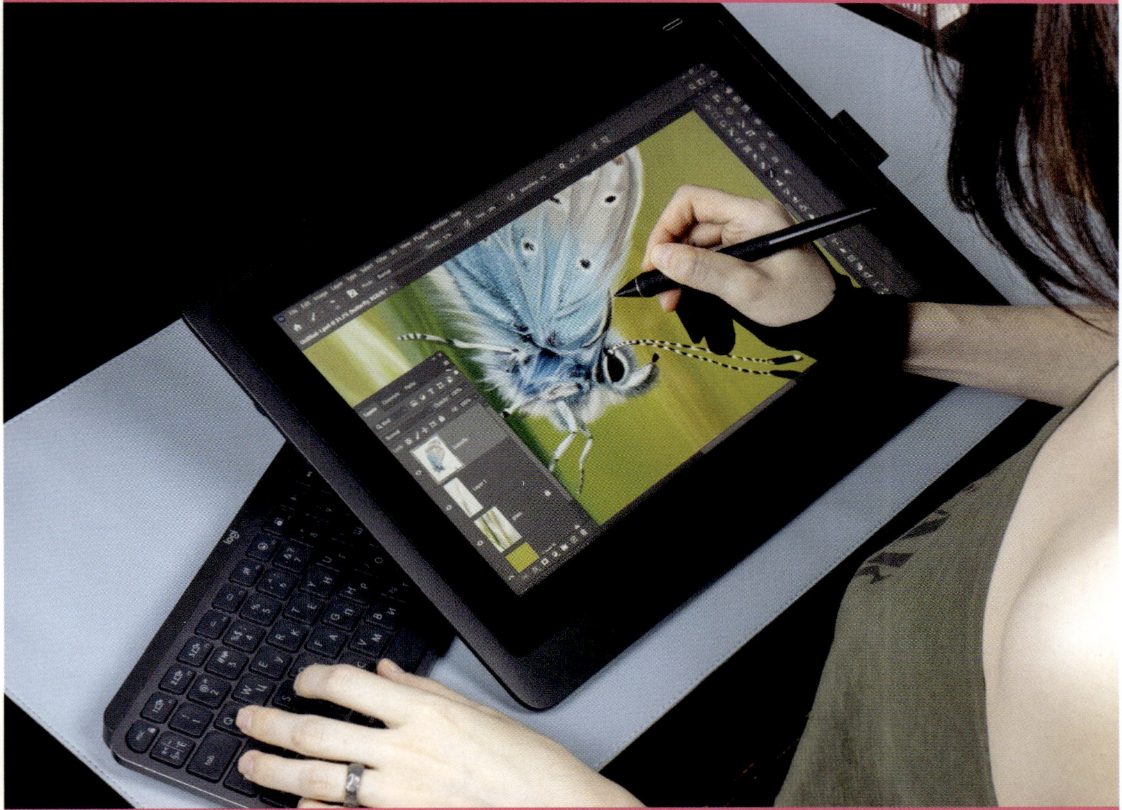

In today's publishing world, illustrators need skills in creating digital art.

Chapter Four

Illustrators as Artists and Businesspeople

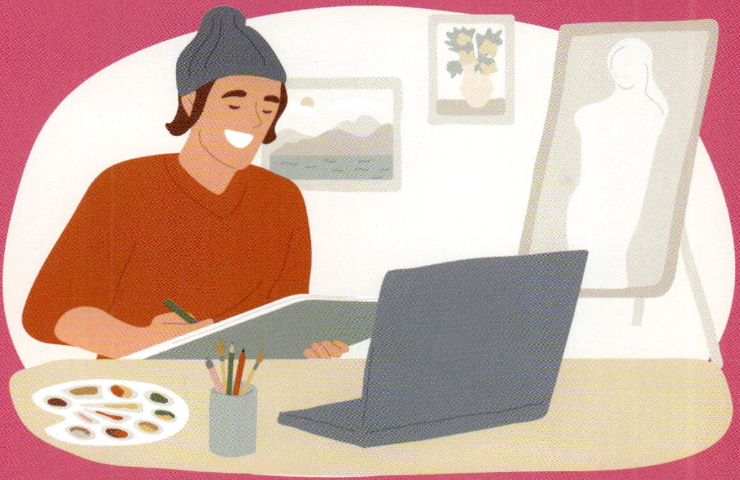

In addition to being artists, most illustrators are businesspeople. They divide their time between making art and running their illustration businesses. Some illustrators are employees of a company. But most illustrators work as freelancers. That means clients hire them to work on individual projects. These clients could be editors or art directors for books or magazines. They could also be people who work in advertising. Some authors who want to publish their own books hire illustrators.

CHAPTER FOUR

Illustrators and clients agree on details such as the fee and a timeline for each project. The details are written in a contract. The client pays the illustrator when the project is finished. This means that most illustrators' income is not regular. And most freelancers do not get health insurance, paid time off, or an office to work in. They must plan for these needs themselves.

Freelancers must find clients. They will need to meet deadlines and fulfill the client's expectations. Communication usually happens through exchanging emails and digital files. Clients will give feedback and request changes. Ordering supplies and managing business finances such as taxes are also part of freelancing.

Some illustrators have additional ways to make money. This helps when they are between illustration projects. They may sell prints of their art. Like Beatrix Potter, some artists turn their work into products such as stickers, posters, games, or stuffed toys. Illustrators may also teach classes or give talks about their work.

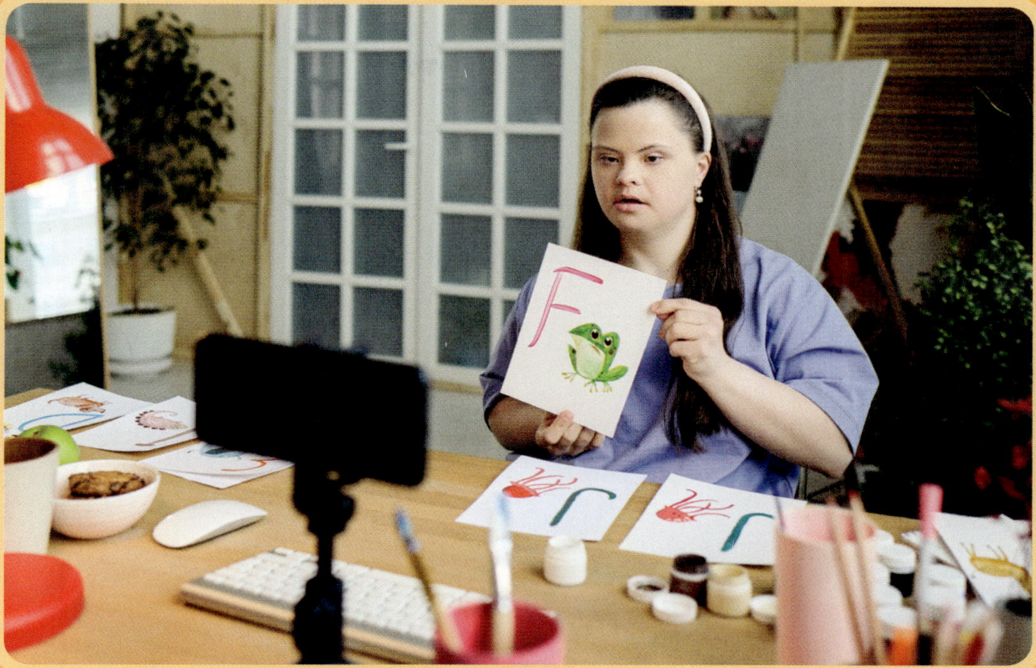

YouTube for Illustrators

For some artists, YouTube can be a source of income. For example, the Art for Kids Hub channel has more than eight million subscribers. For other artists, YouTube is a place to find free education. Many channels offer lessons on specific illustration **techniques**, media, and styles.

While they build a career, many illustrators also work separate jobs. Dow Phumiruk was a doctor before becoming an illustrator and author of children's books. In an interview for this book, she shared, "Many of us continue our day jobs to maintain income **stability**. . . . I teach medical students part-time."

On any given day, illustrators will perform many tasks. They might review a contract or answer an email from a client. They may add a new picture to their portfolio or buy some paints. Their to-do list might also include preparing a talk for a conference. Creating art is just one part of the job.

Illustrators as Artists and Businesspeople

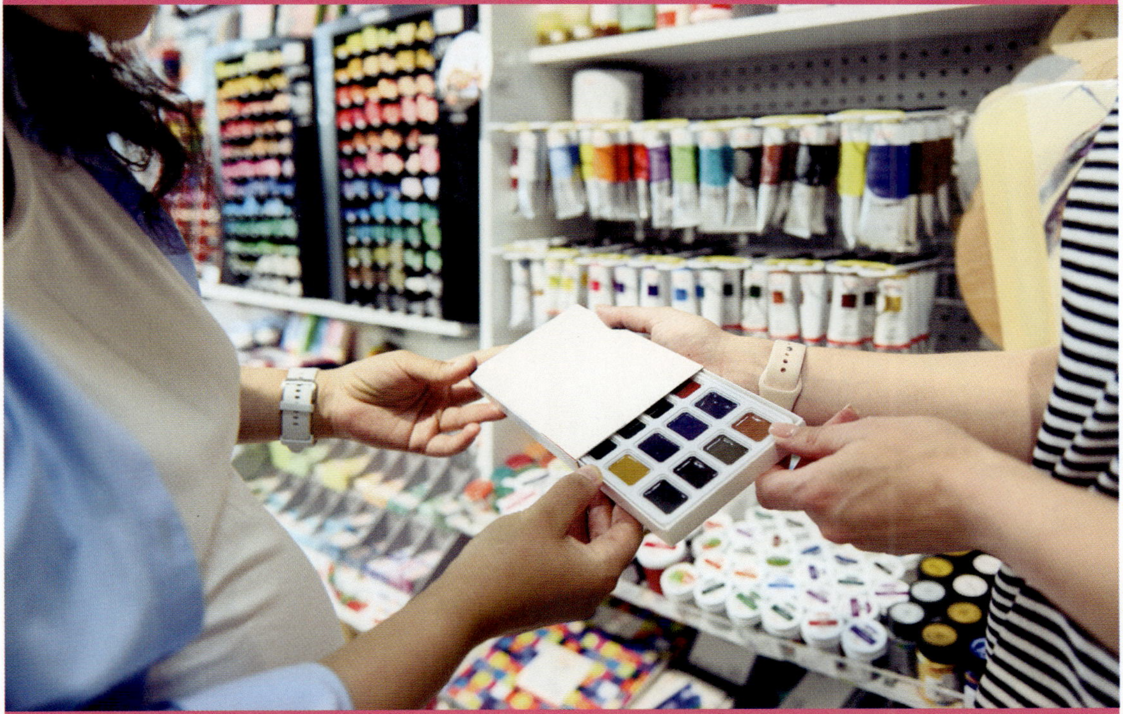

As freelancers, illustrators must plan for the time and cost of buying supplies.

Chapter Five

Getting Started in Illustration

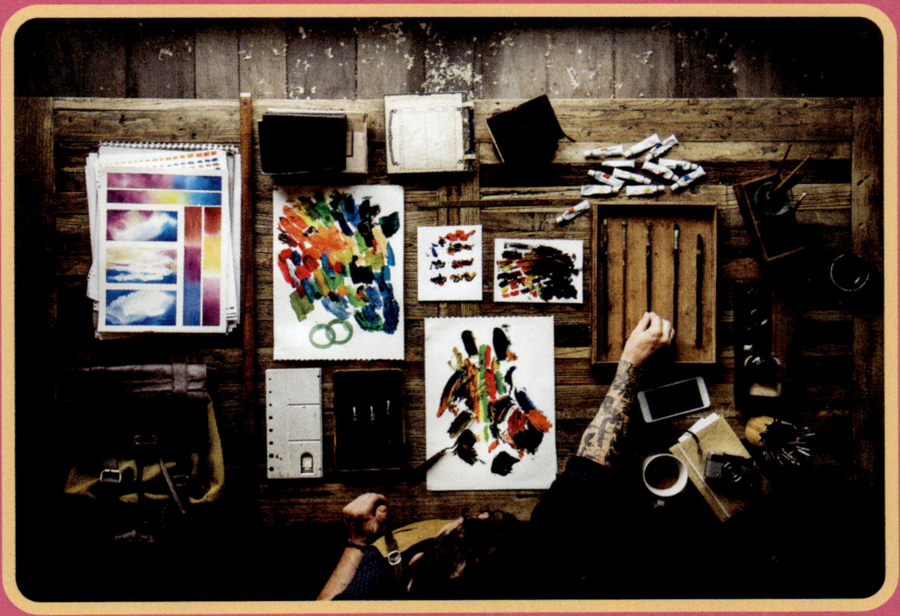

The first step in going from an **amateur** artist to a professional illustrator is building a portfolio. Potential clients almost always want to see a portfolio. Illustrators typically feature between twelve and fifteen works in this collection. The items should highlight the illustrator's **specialties** and interests. For example, someone who wants to illustrate children's books would likely include drawings of children, animals, or other story characters.

CHAPTER FIVE

Even students who may not start working as illustrators for years can make portfolios. These collections can help show the artists' growth and help them further develop their styles. Also, portfolios are usually required to apply to art schools.

Having both paper and digital portfolios is helpful. The digital portfolio can be made into a website to reach new clients. Anyone who sees the website can get in touch with the illustrator through an email address or phone number in the contact section. Some websites feature portfolios from numerous illustrators. These sites let clients consider different artists for projects. However, the sites may charge illustrators or clients for this service.

Social media is another way to find clients and connect with other artists. It can also help grow an audience for illustrators who work in publishing. And it is free to use.

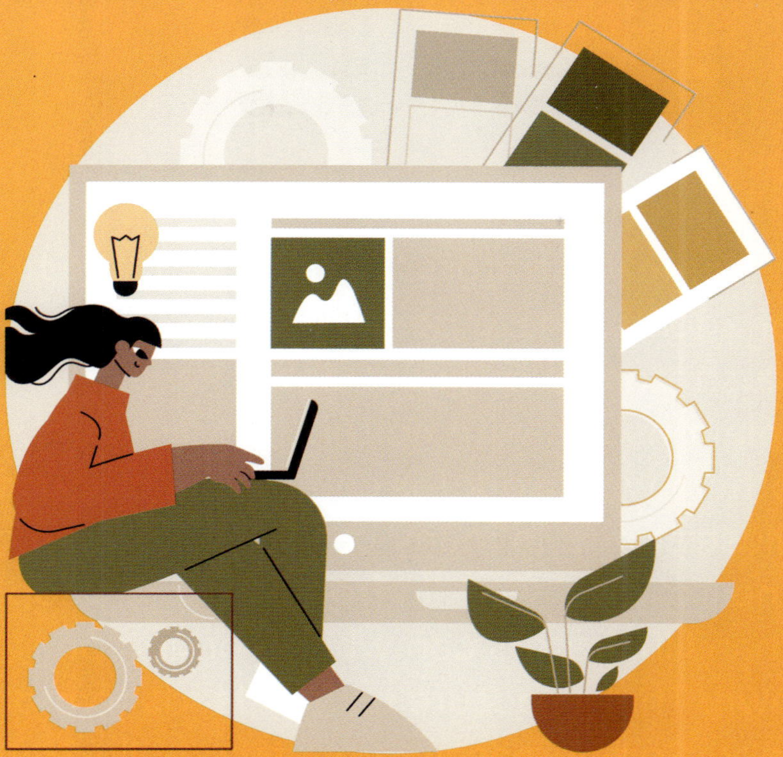

Inspiring Work

Websites that feature many artists' portfolios are more than a way to find jobs. Illustrators can also view other artists' portfolios on these sites. This can be a great way to learn what styles and techniques are common in the field. Viewing other illustrators' portfolios can also be a useful step in making their own work stand out from the competition.

CHAPTER FIVE

Some illustrators find jobs with the help of agents. These people, who represent illustrators in business deals, have relationships with editors, art directors, and others who work for companies that use illustrations. In many cases, agents can get their clients' work in front of more people than illustrators can while working on their own. That exposure usually leads to more jobs. Sometimes agents can get illustrators higher fees or more time to get work done. Agents also review the details of contracts. In exchange, the agent gets a part of the fee for the illustrator's job. Agents are very selective. Many of them will work only with experienced illustrators.

Getting Started in Illustration

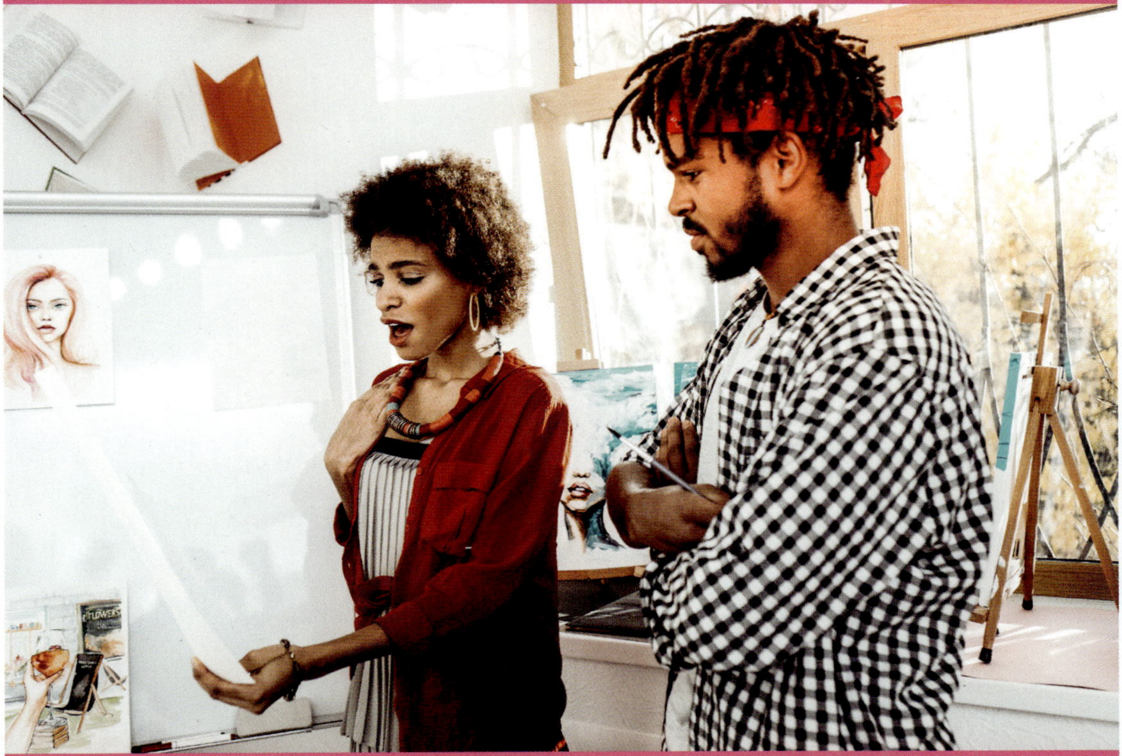

Agents give illustrators feedback and help them find jobs in exchange for part of the fees they earn.

Some professionals advise new illustrators to spend time in a hub for their work. This is an area where many artists work. Being close to other people in the industry can lead to better connections. Fashion illustrator Danielle Meder talked about this in an interview for *Format* magazine. "You don't know who you're going to bump into—it could be somebody who changes your life. That's happened to me several times."

For publishing in the United States, hubs are major cities such as New York, Los Angeles, and Chicago. Fashion illustrators might go to Paris. Courtroom illustrators will work in courts where high-profile cases are tried. That usually means a large city.

Getting Started in Illustration

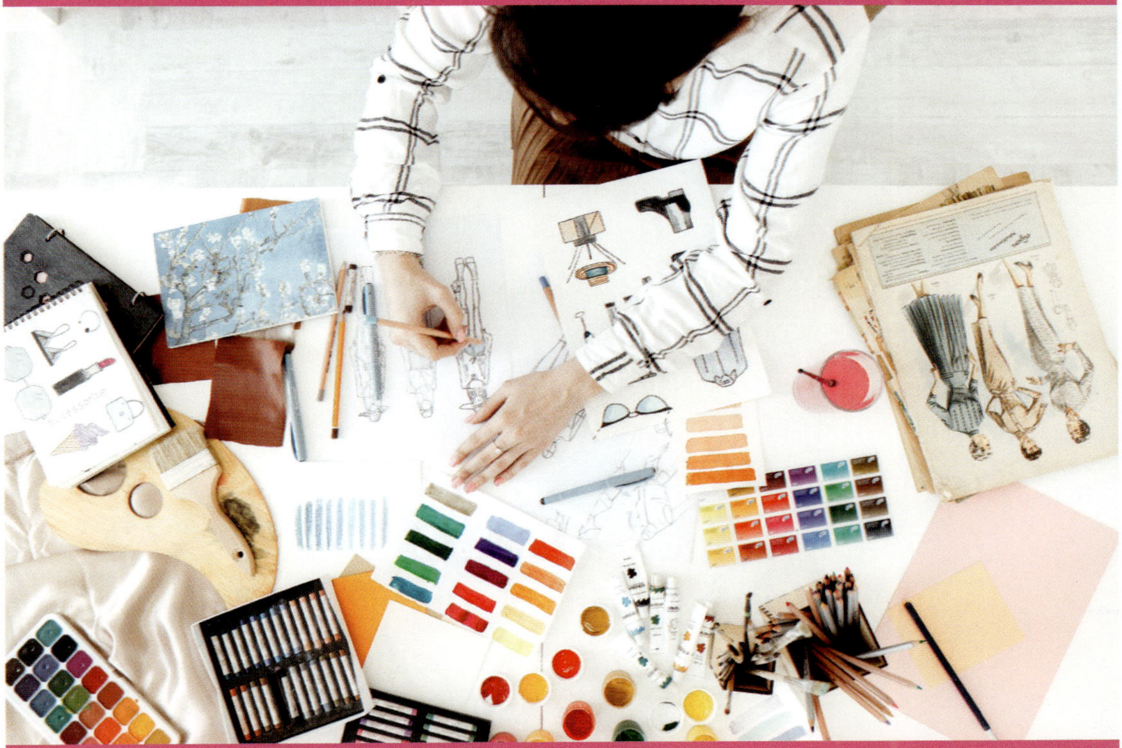

Living or spending time in a city with an active fashion industry can help fashion illustrators find work.

Every job counts for new illustrators. Each one is an opportunity to show they are professional and easy to work with as well as skilled artists. Jobs that go well can lead to repeat clients and **referrals**. Each job also expands an illustrator's experience and portfolio.

Artists who have a passion for storytelling often enjoy a career in illustration. But they must be persistent. It can take years to build a profitable business. But for many illustrators, it is a labor of love. When asked for her advice for young illustrators, Dow Phumiruk shares, "Keep at it until you're noticed. Enjoy yourself as you keep learning about [the] craft, stretching your imagination, and discovering your strengths. Artists create because we can't see ourselves not creating."

Getting Started in Illustration

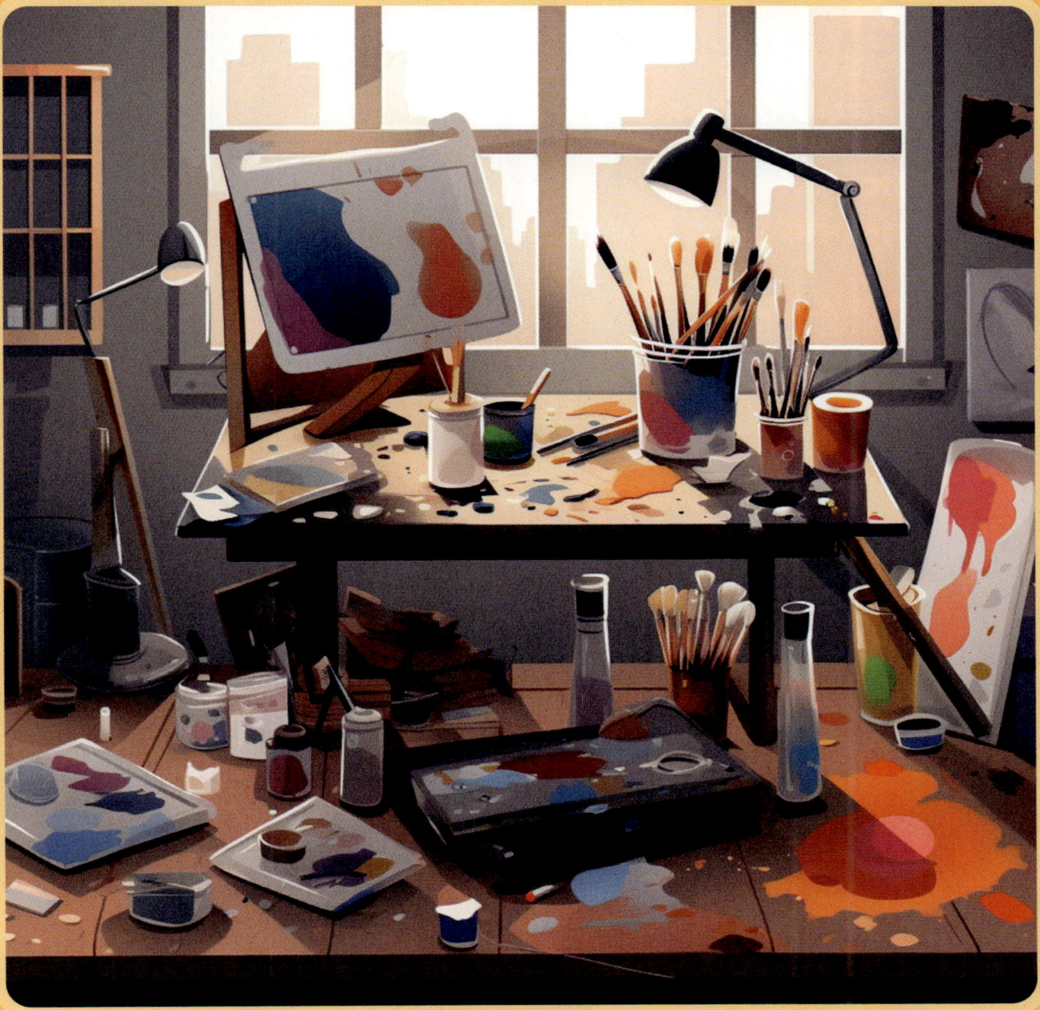

For many illustrators, creating art is more than a job—it is a source of joy and a way to connect with the world.

Glossary

amateur
A person who takes part in an activity for fun and not for payment

bibliophile
Someone who loves books

commissions
Assignments given to artists to create specific works

depicted
Shown by a picture

entrepreneur
A person who opens a business at great financial risk

illustration
Drawings or paintings that appear in publications such as books

media
The tools and materials artists use, such as oil paints or pencils

portfolio
A sampling of an artist's best work

referrals
Suggestions to hire a person made by someone who was pleased with the person's work

specialties
Areas of exceptional skill or training

stability
The ability to remain constant or unchanged

techniques
Skills and talent for a particular activity

Ready, Set, Illustrate!

Test your new knowledge of illustration by answering the following questions.

1. **The Caldecott Medal is awarded yearly for excellence in illustration for:**
   - **A.** Children's literature
   - **B.** Fashion magazines
   - **C.** Medical textbooks

2. **A college art degree:**
   - **A.** Is necessary to become an illustrator
   - **B.** Is a waste of time for someone interested in illustrating
   - **C.** Isn't necessary but can be helpful for finding work as an illustrator

3. **Most illustrators work:**
   - **A.** For large publishing companies
   - **B.** For small publishing companies
   - **C.** As freelancers

4. **How many items do most illustrators feature in a portfolio?**
   - **A.** 7 to 10
   - **B.** 12 to 15
   - **C.** 21 to 24

Answers: A, C, C, B

Find Out More

IN PRINT

Burrows, Ruth. *The Illustrator's Guide to Procreate*. David & Charles, 2023.

Helt, Julianna. *A Career in Cartooning*. Mitchell Lane Publishers, 2026.

Watt, Fiona. *Step-by-Step Drawing Animals*. Usborne, 2024.

ON THE INTERNET

Association of Medical Illustrations.
https://ami.org/medical-illustration/enter-the-profession

Das, Bidisha. "How to Become an Illustrator in 4 Steps (with FAQs)," *Indeed*, August 18, 2024.
www.indeed.com/career-advice/finding-a-job/how-to-become-illustrator

The Society of Children's Book Writers and Illustrators.
www.scbwi.org

Index

About the Author

Rachel Bithell writes fiction and nonfiction for kids and their caregivers. Her debut novel, *Brave Bird at Wounded Knee: A Story of Protest on the Pine Ridge Indian Reservation*, won a Colorado Book Award. She is also a teacher who loves to see kids dive into things they love. If you love art, she wishes you the best of luck following your passion!